TODAY
IS
YOURS

Other Books by Pat Williams

TODAY
IS
YOURS

DAILY INSPIRATION
FOR SUCCESS

PAT WILLIAMS

WITH JIM DENNEY

SPIRE

© 2014 by Baker Publishing Group

Published by Revell
a division of Baker Publishing Group
P.O. Box 6287, Grand Rapids, MI 49516-6287
www.revellbooks.com

ISBN 978-0-8007-2373-6

Printed in the United States of America

14   15   16   17   18   19   20   7   6   5   4   3   2   1

To Dr. Warren Wiersbe, my pastor at
Moody Memorial Church
in Chicago in the early 1970s
and a good friend for many decades since.

Contents

CONTENTS

Foreword

Dr. Bill Sutton, university professor and NBA consultant, calls Pat Williams "this generation's Mark Twain." I think of Pat as this generation's Walt Disney. Both Pat and Walt envisioned extreme dreams, then assembled teams to make their dreams come true. Both built magical entertainment empires in Orlando, Florida.

People told Pat Williams he was crazy to try to bring NBA basketball to Orlando, a town without any pro sports tradition. It turns out he *was* crazy—as crazy as Steve Jobs, the visionary behind Apple computers; as crazy as Gutzon Borglum, who carved the faces on Mount Rushmore; as crazy as Joseph Strauss, who built the Golden Gate Bridge.

What is your dream? People may call you crazy, but Pat will tell you how to make your dreams come true. In this book, we've adapted 365 of his most life-changing insights from five books we wrote for Revell—*A Lifetime of Success, Ahead of the Game, Coach Wooden, Coach Wooden's Greatest Secret,* and *The Difference You Make*.

Immerse yourself in the wisdom and enthusiasm of this man who has impacted my life in countless ways. Today is yours—and it's going to be *awesome*!

—Jim Denney

1

Character

1

We build character by the choices we make.

2

Every time we resist temptation, stand
firm under pressure, or act selflessly,
our character grows stronger.

3

Some people define *character* as "what you do when nobody is looking." True enough. But character also means doing the right thing when people want you to do wrong. Standing against peer pressure is also an unmistakable sign of character.

4

I define *character* as "who we are when we are tested by temptation or adversity."

5

For good or ill, character is the result
of the habits we acquire over time.

6

Character begins with a decision.

7

Character is becoming an increasingly rare
commodity in our world—and that means
character is more important than ever.

8

A person's inner reality should match
his or her outer reputation. If not,
that person is a walking lie.

9

This world needs people who tell the
truth, even when there's a price to pay.

10

We need more people who prize personal
honor above momentary gain.

11

Your character is the sum total of
your enduring moral attributes.

12

Every morally sound decision
contributes to stronger character.

13

A person of character is incorruptible.
Why? Because a dishonest act
would violate his self-image.

14

The accumulation of all of our moral decisions stamps a pattern onto our lives. This pattern is called *character*.

15

Be true to yourself and you'll never be false to others.

16

You can fake a reputation but you can't fake character.

17

There is no such thing as a small
lapse of character. We either
have integrity or we don't.

18

Build trust by practicing integrity.
When in doubt, always tell the truth.

19

Dishonesty destroys influence. Our
influence is built on a foundation
of ethical behavior and truth.

20

Coach John Wooden didn't consider himself too important to do "little jobs" like sweeping the gym floor.

21

The most humble people I've met generally have the most dynamic and impressive personalities.

22

Humility is one of the most attractive qualities any human being can possess.

23

When a person of genuine humility comes
along, the whole world takes notice.

24

If you maintain your moral character in
the little things, you'll never have your
reputation destroyed by the big things.

25

By guarding your character in the
little things, you make sure you can
be trusted with the big things.

26

Few of us realize the awesome
power we possess through the
power to make moral choices.

27

If you're never caught taking a paper
clip from your employer's office, you'll
never go to prison for embezzlement.

28

We like to think we're "good people." But if
we searchingly examined all the corners and
crevices of our lives, what would we find?

29

Every "little sin" is a skirmish in a
never-ending struggle for control of
this battlefield called our souls.

30

Every day, we are bombarded by choices.
Every hour, we are required to make
moral decisions. Our character is made
up of these seemingly "little" choices.

31

Little nicks and flaws in our
character can cause big trouble.

32

Most of us give ourselves more credit
for character than we deserve.

33

Until we have sterling character in the
"little things" of life, we can't claim
to be people of character at all.

34

Never mistake reputation for
character. If our reputation exceeds
our character, we are hypocrites.

35

Each decision we make helps to cement
the kind of people we will be.

36

Don't yield to circumstances. Don't
yield to opponents. Don't yield to
critics. Endure—and outlast them all,
as the anvil outlasts the hammer.

37

You are capable of far more than
you imagine. If you keep pursuing
your passion, you will triumph.

38

Courage is the healthy management of
our fears. It's not cowardly to be afraid.
It's only cowardly to be controlled by
fear. When we control fear instead of
letting fear control us, that's courage.

39

If you fail, get up and get after
that dream again and again.

40

Greatness is the result of character.

41

Patience isn't complacency. Patience is
the willingness to wait until just the right
moment. Don't act too soon or too late. Wait
until the opportunity ripens—then *act*.

42

True wisdom is a deep understanding
of what is true, right, and lasting.

43

Many of the smartest people in the
world are sadly lacking in wisdom.

44

Knowledge likes to speak; wisdom prefers to listen. Knowledge studies; wisdom observes. Knowledge knows how to take things apart; wisdom understands how to put things back together. Knowledge is proud of all it has learned; wisdom is humble and thirsts to learn more.

45

People of greatness don't care who gets the credit. They just want to lift others up.

46

I've often thought of the words of business leader Holbrook Jackson: "When in doubt, risk it!" I did—and I have no regrets.

47

Seek advice. Ask for help. Serve your apprenticeship. Accept coaching with a patient, eager, hungry-to-learn attitude— then be a mentor and teacher to others.

48

I decided early in life that I didn't want
to have any regrets. I figured life is a
smorgasbord, and I was going to have a
taste of everything before I was done.

49

Work hard. Be willing to sacrifice ease
and pleasure to win what really counts.

50

Mr. R. E. Littlejohn used to tell me, "The man who rows the boat generally doesn't have time to rock it." So put in the hours, gain your experience, and pay your dues.

51

If you want a lifetime of success, nothing beats hard work.

52

Millions have seen Michael Jordan, the
finished product, working miracles on the
court. But few have seen how that product
was built by hours of sweat, pain, and
grueling exertion on the practice floor.

53

No one becomes Michael Jordan without
leaving a trail of sweat—not even Michael
Jordan. He didn't get to the top of his
game by being a natural-born athlete.
He got there by being Mr. Work Ethic.

54

Avoid condemning or judging others. Those who assign blame are thinking Win/Lose, not Win/Win. What good does it do to make the other person a "loser"? Why not resolve the conflict so you both can win?

2

Competing
and Winning

55

Winning is not the objective;
winning is a byproduct.

56

Winning is the result of preparation, a strong
work ethic, and attention to the little things.

57

Anyone can say, "Our goal is to win the
championship." But champions say, "We're
going to eliminate all the little mistakes
that could cost us the championship."

58

Our goal is the relentless pursuit
of excellence. You can never
quite achieve perfection, but you
never cease reaching for it.

59

As Bill Veeck said, "The best
promotion is winning."

60

When Irv Kosloff was the owner of the
Philadelphia 76ers, he told me, "Ask
yourself two questions every hour of the
day. First: What am I doing to help the
team win more games? Second: What am
I doing to draw more fans? Remember
those two questions and you'll never get
sidetracked." I follow that advice to this day.

61

The pursuit of excellence begins
with attention to the little things.

62

Only mediocre people consider
excellence to be the exception. To
successful people, excellence is a habit.

63

NBA coach Chuck Daly once told me, "Ours is a suffering business, because at the end of the year, everybody is suffering except one team." It's true. The best teams go to the playoffs, and every team but one ends the season with a spirit-crushing loss. Only one team celebrates at the end. A suffering business indeed.

64

Never settle for second best. "Good enough" is never good enough.

3

Faith

65

God created us as material and spiritual
beings. If we focus only on our material
well-being and forget the spiritual,
we'll be left unsatisfied. That's the
message of Ecclesiastes 5:10: "Whoever
loves money never has enough."

66

In 1968, I made a decision to dig everything
I could out of the Bible. That book
transformed my life as I have read it, studied
it, and memorized passages from it.

67

There is no true success apart from a
relationship with God. I was twenty-
seven when I made this discovery,
and I only wish I had been seven.

68

Life is awesome. God is awesome.

69

To me, Christianity isn't a religion.
Christianity is Christ.

70

Jesus is relevance personified. He
is gutsy, contemporary, strong, and
real. He is the Friend I depend on
in my world of ups and downs.

71

I once gave a talk in church on Mao Tse-
Tung's "Four Absolutes," his plan for
capturing the world for communism.
Those "Four Absolutes" make a great
basis for living out the Christian faith:
absolute acceptance, absolute dedication,
absolute discipline, and absolute action.
If more Christians were as serious about
Jesus as the Chinese communists were
about their ideology, Christianity would
be a stronger force in the world.

72

To hear the still, small voice of God's
Spirit, we must stop and listen.

73

Many people treat prayer as a last resort:
"Well, I guess there's nothing left to
do but pray." If we want to influence
others, we must begin with prayer.

74

The God I know is a God
of Second Chances.

75

The Christian life is warfare—and a grand adventure in a great cause.

76

When you are sustained by the prayers of God's people, you can tell something supernatural is taking place in your life, in your spirit, in your emotions, and in the cells of your body.

77

Prayer is influence.

78

When you are thankful for your blessings,
more blessings flow your way.

79

Grateful people are happy people. They look
for pleasure in simple blessings. They focus
on what they *have* instead of what they *want*.

80

Learn to view the good things in your
life as blessings, not entitlements.

81

Practice saying "thank you." Thank the
mailman and the clerk at the grocery
store. Astonish your boss by thanking
him for your job. If *you* are the boss,
thank your employees for working hard
to make your business successful.

82

Gratitude does as much good for those
who give it as for those who receive it.

83

Before you roll out of bed, thank
God for the new day.

4

Family

84

My father, Jim Williams, was always taking snapshots, shooting home movies, hollering at my games, and telling everybody, "That's my boy!" I was lucky to be so loved, and I wish I had appreciated it more at the time.

85

Family time is sacred time.
Guard it like a bulldog.

86

A parent's influence lasts a lifetime.

87

There are few greater ways to bless and affirm your children than by saying, "I'm proud of you."

88

How do children spell "love"? They spell it T-I-M-E.

89

I remember sitting with Mom while she
read aloud to me when I was little. She's
the reason I'm such a compulsive reader to
this day. Mom often took us to New York
and Philadelphia to visit museums, attend
concerts, go to the zoo, and watch Broadway
shows. My friend, Jerry Jenkins, calls me
a "renaissance jock." I owe it all to Mom.

90

As my kids became teenagers, I noticed
they don't come to me very much
anymore. If I wanted to have a relationship
with them, I had to go to them.

91

I have been in the delivery room to welcome
four birth-children into the Williams clan.
I have also stood in the airport terminal
to welcome fourteen adopted children
into the Williams clan. I have kissed and
blessed each one of those kids, and I have
told them about a loving God who has
a wonderful future planned for them.

92

A parent's love is stronger and more
important than biology. To me, a "parent" is
anyone who has the spiritual and emotional
capacity to love and nurture a child.

93

When people ask how many children I have,
I say, "Nineteen—four birth children, one
by remarriage, and fourteen by international
adoption . . . but I forget which fourteen."

94

Share stories from your own experience
with your children. Even if they groan
and give you a hard time, they want to
compare their own lives with yours.

95

Prophesy a great future for your
children. Let them know you
love them unconditionally.

96

I'm a deeply flawed human being—flawed
as a husband, as a father, and as a Christian.
I am the father of nineteen flawed human
beings. We've had our share of problems,
but there was always a nucleus of love,
faith, and commitment that bonded us.
I believe our miniature United Nations
succeeded because we were committed to
living out love, acceptance, and forgiveness.

97

Enjoy being with your kids, and
they will enjoy being with you.

98

Be consistent. Be firm. Be
loving. And *be the parent*.

99

Kids need limits. They crave structure—
even when they rebel against it. Children
need limits on television, computer
games, and other entertainment, and they
need a set time for doing homework.

100

When investing time in our kids, let's invest our full attention. That means making eye contact, listening, giving verbal feedback, and enjoying those fleeting moments when we can influence their lives.

101

Don't just *say* you love your spouse and kids. *Prove* it with the gift of your time.

102

If you lose your temper, you'll lose
control of the situation—and that's
why kids often provoke their parents.
When you remain calm and rational,
you prove you're in control.

103

Give your children opportunities to build
character by serving others. Encourage
them to wash windows or pull weeds
for an elderly neighbor—not to make
money, but to make a difference.

104

We applied for a pair of boys from Korea.
In the pictures they looked lonely and
sad beneath unruly mops of black hair.
"Why aren't they smiling?" asked one of
our children. I said, "When they have a
home to belong to, you'll see them smile."

105

No one ever wrote a manual on how to raise
a family like ours. I carry around a mental
image of one of my children standing up
and saying, "I'm honored to accept this
Nobel Peace Prize on behalf of humanity."
But there are also times I imagine that same
child saying, "You want fries with that?"

106

Both partners must be 100 percent
committed to keeping a marriage
healthy. It's not good enough to say,
"Marriage is 50-50—I'm doing my half."
Marriage is a 100-100 proposition. The
50-50 mindset leads many couples to
draw a line down the middle of their
relationship. Divide a marriage in half
and you're halfway to divorce.

107

God in his mercy will sometimes pick up the pieces of our lives and put them back together in new and surprising ways. It happened in my life. But before God put my life back together, I went through the worst emotional pain of my life. Until you've been through it, you have no idea how much it hurts.

108

My wife Ruth and I started as friends.
Today we are soul mates. She loves the
Lord, she's as passionate about life as I am,
and she loves sports. Forget the "opposites
attract" stuff. She and I are alike in every
way except gender (vive *that* différence!).

109

Ruth and I were babysitting our three-year-old grandson, Anthony. I needed something from my car, so I headed for the door—then I heard a little voice behind me: "Poppers, where are you going?"

I said, "I'm going to my car, Anthony."

"Can I follow you?"

"Sure, Anthony, sure."

As he followed me to the car, he said, "Poppers, can I follow you all the time?"

"Sure you can."

"Wherever you go?"

"Yes, wherever I go."

At that moment, I felt a lump in my throat. I was overwhelmed by the joy—and the responsibility— of influencing future generations.

5

Finances

110

If you accumulate enough pennies,
you'll eventually be rich.

111

Beware the warning signs of out-of-
control finances: an inability to pay your
bills on time; an inability to save; maxed
out credit cards; and arguments with
your spouse over money. Live within
your means and build net worth.

112

When you buy new clothes or a new lamp,
leave the tags on for a week and keep your
receipts. See if you really want to keep
your new purchase. If not, take it back.

113

Finances are ultimately a spiritual issue.
Two-thirds of the parables of Jesus deal
with finances. He constantly warned
against greed, pride, and coveting.

114

We see greed manifested when people go into debt to acquire things they can't afford and haven't earned.

115

When a company that operates on sound moral principles makes a profit, good things happen: (1) the company produces goods or services that benefit society; (2) it provides honorable employment at a just wage; (3) it treats employees with dignity; (4) it pays its bills, which grows the economy; and (5) it's a good corporate citizen, making charitable contributions for the betterment of society. Failure benefits nobody; success benefits everybody.

116

Being successful doesn't necessarily mean being wealthy.

117

A world in which no one could make
a profit would be a world of misery
and poverty, without food, medicine,
entertainment, transportation, goods
and services, technology, science,
education, or any of the other wonderful
things that result from people who want
to succeed and earn a good living.

118

There's nothing wrong with profit. But if
your concept of "success" begins and ends
with material gain, you're destined to fail.

6

Fun

119

One thing I like about pro basketball
is the noise. A loud crowd can
rock the roof off the house.

120

Circus clowns and I are in roughly the
same business. I'd be right at home in
a rubber nose, frizzy wig, and size 90
shoes. Clowns live to help people forget
their troubles for a while. So do I.

121

Bill Veeck once told me, "You're in the entertainment business, and don't ever apologize for it."

122

"Be accessible," Bill Veeck once said. "Don't screen your calls. Don't screen your mail. Let people see you and talk to you, let them grab you by the lapels and tell you what they think. Stand at the exits after the game and thank them for coming. Don't sell the games on the won and lost column—that's too risky. Instead, guarantee your fans a good time and lots of fun." I never forgot those words.

7

Get the Job
or Promotion

123

Sell yourself. Be confident and show yourself to be dependable and trustworthy.

124

The job doesn't always go to the person most qualified. It generally goes to the one best prepared.

125

Employers see many candidates with similar
levels of education, experience, and other
qualifications on their résumé. There will
probably not be one big thing to set you
apart. The employer will probably make
a decision based on a lot of little things
that take place during the interview.

126

Mediocre achievers are content
with mediocre preparation.

127

One of the best ways to give yourself
an edge is to arrive early.

128

You never have to make an
excuse for being early.

129

Prepare yourself for the day your coach calls
your number and sends you into the game.
Someday, your chance will come. Be ready.

130

If you make a mistake, admit it. People
think more highly of those who apologize
than those who make excuses.

131

A cluttered environment
produces cluttered thinking.

132

Don't just meet your boss's
expectations—amaze her.

133

Come in earlier, stay later, work
harder, offer more value, attract more
clients, and generate more glowing
reviews than anyone expected.

134

If you exceed expectations, your boss
will become your biggest booster.

8

Goals and Success

135

From the time I saw my first Major
League Baseball game at age seven,
I dreamed of a career in professional
sports. The dream never let me down.

136

As a seven-year-old, I set goals for my
life. I bought into the American game
plan of finding out what you enjoy in
life, setting that as a goal, and pursuing
it with everything you've got.

137

The grades you earn in school are less important than the effort you expend to get those grades. People who work their tails off for a C-plus usually achieve greater success in life than those who coast effortlessly to an A.

138

Find the one passion that thrills and energizes you—then invest your life in it.

139

Make sure you rule your passion—
don't let it rule you.

140

When I'm on a mission, I'm unstoppable.
That's my great strength in life—
and, at times, my great weakness.

141

Successful people may not like rising
early, working hard, and staying
late, but they know that's the price
for surpassing mediocrity.

142

There's no big secret to success.
There are only a lot of little things
that add up to a slight edge.

143

What is the secret of success? There is
no secret! Vast rewards accrue to those
who put out a little extra effort.

144

The rewards go to the best prepared.

145

If we live out God's purpose for our lives,
how can we be anything but successful?

146

A basketball game is a series of small
skirmishes. A book is a stack of pages
written one sentence at a time. The
successful achievement of any goal is the
result of a lot of little things done well.

147

To be successful, be consistent
in the little things.

148

Never settle for living in the gray areas of
life. Reach for some magnificent goal.

149

If you fail, make sure you fail valiantly,
so that all the world will marvel at your
courage in making the attempt.

150

Failure is never final unless you quit.

151

Opportunities belong to those who reach
for them; they rarely fall into your lap.

152

Write down your goals, post them in a
visible place, and review them often.

153

A little extra effort can make
a big impression.

154

Luck is fine, but most successful people
make their own luck by persevering
through obstacles and setbacks.

155

The way to success is usually a ladder,
not an elevator. Keep climbing.

156

No one's life moves in a straight line. You
have to flex when life zigs and zags.

157

Roy Disney, Walt Disney's brother and business partner, once said, "When your values are clear to you, making decisions becomes easier." It's true. Good principles dictate good decisions.

158

Delegating responsibility has never been my strong suit. Over my years in professional sports, it gradually dawned on me that I had to trust other people to get the job done.

159

The fear of delegating is a sign of insecurity.
The more confident I felt in my job, the
more comfortable I became with delegating.

160

What do you want to sell? A message?
An idea? A product? It all starts with
you. You must sell you. You must
make a great first impression.

161

The fundamentals of selling are: (1) get
your client's attention; (2) convert
attention into interest; (3) convert interest
into conviction; (4) convert conviction
into desire; and (5) close the deal.

162

Great salespeople are fanatically
dedicated to pleasing their customers.

163

Your primary objective is not to make
a sale, but to make customers.

164

Focus on the customer, listen to him,
make him the center of your attention.
People love to talk about themselves, so
get your customer to talk about herself
and her needs. Then show her how
your product meets those needs.

165

Selling is more than pitching a product. It's
spinning a dream and helping people to
visualize themselves enjoying that dream.

166

Empathize. You can't be successful focusing only on your own wants and needs.

167

Make yourself and your product indispensable to your customers.

168

You will succeed if you maintain consistency in the little things.

169

At the end of each day, ask yourself, "What
did I accomplish today? What could I
have done better? Did I advance closer to
my goals? Did I stick to my priorities?"

170

A habit of reviewing the day's
accomplishments and planning the
next day's priorities is a powerful
tool for reaching your goals.

9

Habits

171

We are the sum of the habits
we build over a lifetime.

172

We are what we repeatedly do.

173

The best way to break a bad habit is
to replace it with a good habit.

174

We are creatures of habit, and our habits
define who we are—for better or worse.

10

Health and Fitness

175

Just prior to my fiftieth birthday, I saw
a newspaper article about Hank Henry,
who bench-pressed 350 pounds on his
sixty-fifth birthday. So I started pumping
iron. Nobody has mistaken me for Charles
Atlas yet, but I've never felt better, and
I love the idea of improving with age.

176

I intend to outrun, outlift, and outdo my
grandkids when I'm into my eighties.

177

Exercise strengthens the body
and sharpens the mind.

178

Being overweight is expensive. Getting
into shape can save you money on medical
expenses, life insurance, and lost work.

179

When it's time to relax, *relax*.

180

Life is a marathon. You have to pace yourself in order to go the distance.

181

Dr. Reynolds said, "It's definite, Pat. You have multiple myeloma."

"How curable is it?"

"It's not curable, but it's treatable. The goal is remission."

At that point, I had an inspiration. I said, "How about this for a motivational slogan? 'The Mission is Remission.'"

11

Influence

182

Great people lift us up and carry us on their shoulders to heights we could never reach on our own.

183

Your children notice when you break the speed limit. Your employees notice when you lie to customers. Your co-workers notice when you cheat on your expense account. Live as if you are under a microscope. You are.

184

We all impact the people around
us—and we have all been impacted
by the influencers in our own lives.

185

We all make a difference in the lives of
others. The only question is: What kind
of difference do we choose to make?

186

I was general manager of the Spartanburg
Phillies from 1965 to 1968, and the owner,
Mr. R. E. Littlejohn, became my mentor
and best friend. Looking back, I can see
my younger self as he must have seen
me: impetuous, impatient, and rough
around the edges. My attitude was, "I
want everything, and I want it now!"

187

Mr. Littlejohn loved my enthusiasm, but he
knew I lacked maturity. So he instructed me,
influenced me, and impacted my young life.

188

Most people want to do well; Mr. R. E. Littlejohn wanted to do right. Most people say, "Do what feels good"; Mr. Littlejohn said, "Do good—and you'll never regret it." Most people care about looking good; Mr. R. E. cared about doing good, even when no one was looking.

189

I told Mr. Littlejohn, "We could make more money if we sold beer."

He was horrified. "Pat," he said, "if I we did that, I'd have to sell the team!" He explained that he believed alcohol had a corrupting influence on the young, so he wouldn't allow it on the premises. I learned to always be aware of my influence.

190

Bill Veeck was my mentor, friend, and role model. The lessons he taught me almost five decades ago still shape my decisions to this day.

191

You don't have to be perfect to influence others. You can influence people by the way you recover from your failures.

192

Who are the influencers in *your* life? Who shaped your values and your character? Who enabled you to believe in yourself? You can never pay those people back, but you can "pay it forward" to the young people in your sphere of influence. Who will you impact with your influence today?

193

We tend to underrate our influence.
Our words and actions have more
impact than we realize.

194

Athletes and celebrities are role
models—it's inescapable. They must
choose between wielding *healthy*
influence or *corrosive* influence.

195

The impact of influence begins with an
awareness of our influence. The greater
our awareness, the greater our influence.

196

I eagerly looked forward to my visits
with Coach John Wooden. I wanted
to soak up every atom of his wisdom,
his values, his faith, and the aura of his
personality. I wanted to be like him.
Though I was in my sixties when I first met
him, I wanted him to be proud of me.

197

One of Coach Wooden's chief concerns was excellence. He wanted to raise up a cadre of scholar-athletes—well-rounded individuals who would excel both on and off the court.

198

Great teachers are great simplifiers. They take complex ideas and break them down into their component parts.

199

If you want to influence others, be
a servant. Find a person with dirty
windows—then clean them. Find
someone who is friendless—and be a
friend. Read to a child. Serve meals at
the homeless shelter. Be a servant.

200

We can all be servants. We can all be
mentors. We can all be empowerers. Serving,
mentoring, and empowering are three
ways to impact others with our influence.

201

Whenever we empower the people
around us, we set them up for success.
Empowerment is an elixir for the soul.

202

Most great people have had mentors.

203

Wisdom doesn't come naturally. It must be
learned—either from personal experience
(which is learning the hard way) or
from the example of wise mentors.

204

Mr. Littlejohn mentored me and invested
in me. Day by day, through the things
he showed me and taught me, he made
an incalculable investment in my life.

205

I once heard football coach Gene Stallings
say, "I have yet to see a young person go
wrong who had one good adult friend."

206

In *Pop Warner's Book For Boys*, the great college football coach wrote, "If you're going to be a great athlete, don't drink, don't smoke. Get your rest." I bought into that message as a boy. I wish there were more influences like Pop Warner for kids today.

207

I've been a Ted Williams fan almost as
long as I can remember. I saw him for the
first time at an A's-Red Sox doubleheader
when I was fourteen. Afterwards, Ted
sat in the front of the team bus. Kids
swarmed like mosquitoes in July, clamoring
for his autograph. Ted roared, "If you
guys don't get in line, I'm not signing
autographs!" The kids obeyed and Ted
signed autographs for every kid there,
including an avid young Pat Williams. I still
have that signed photo in my collection.

208

I imitated my baseball heroes. I read that
Rogers Hornsby, the great National League
hitter, never went to the movies because
he believed those flickering pictures
would harm his eyesight. So I avoided
the movies while I was growing up.

209

You don't have to be an NBA star or a
rock star or a four-star general to have
a stellar influence on others. Influence
is a grassroots quality. We all have it.

210

After I went away to college, my old coach, Peanuts Riley, wrote to me and said, "Hustle a little more every day. Don't ever lose your confidence. Remember, the other fellows put their uniforms on the same way you do. Never stop swinging, and you'll be rough on all of them." I kept that letter in my wallet for years.

211

I first met Bill Veeck in 1962 at his home overlooking Chesapeake Bay. He gave me four pieces of advice I've never forgotten. "First," he said, "know somebody. It's almost impossible to get inside professional baseball if you don't know somebody. Second, learn to type. Third, learn all you can about advertising and marketing. Fourth, get some kind of business background." Our friendship lasted until his death in 1986.

212

Since my cancer diagnosis in 2011, I pay
more attention than ever before to the
phone calls, letters, and emails I receive.
I'm aware that some little paragraph I
write back could impact someone's life.

213

We're all under a death sentence. I am
and so are you. Multiple myeloma has
heightened my sense of urgency to
live each day to influence others.

12

Leadership

214

Every leader is in the people business.
Leadership is nothing more or
less than the ability to achieve
goals by influencing people.

215

If you want to gauge a leader's influence,
measure the accomplishments of that
leader's team or organization. The greater
the results, the greater the influence.

216

Leaders can delegate tasks and authority,
but leaders cannot delegate responsibility.
We're responsible for every action and
decision of those under our command.

217

Leaders must care about the
good of individuals, not just the
success of the organization.

218

Leadership is not about being the
boss. It's about being a servant.

219

Don't solve problems for your subordinates.
Your job as a leader is to equip your
people to solve their own problems.

220

The most talented team in the world
can't win without great coaching.

221

I call the fundamental ingredients of leadership "The Seven Sides of Leadership." They are:

1. *Vision*. Successful leaders are visionaries who dream of a brighter future, then lead people toward the fulfillment of that vision.

2. *Communication Skills*. Successful leaders are skilled communicators who are able to convey their vision and energize their people.

3. *People Skills*. Successful leaders know how to make people feel respected, empowered, and valued.

4. *Character*. Successful leaders are people of integrity, courage, hard work, fairness, and good judgment.

5. *Competence*. Successful leaders have the experience and ability to make their teams and organizations competitive.

6. *Boldness*. Successful leaders are decisive and courageous. Their boldness inspires confidence in their people.

7. *A Serving Heart*. Successful leaders are not bosses; they are servants of the people they lead.

222

Take care of the people who work for you, and they will take care of you.

223

Make sure employees feel that their opinions and ideas matter, and that their contributions are valued.

224

Good communication flows from shared goals, shared relationships, and a sense of teamwork.

225

Information flows freely when everyone feels committed to a common good.

226

By paying attention to the little things,
great leaders accomplish big things.

227

Most of us have a pretty good idea
of what we ought to do most of the
time—we just don't want to do it.

228

Act firmly and decisively. Odds are,
you made the right decision.

229

A championship team isn't just a
bunch of guys who can run, shoot, and
hang from the hoop. Championships
are the result of talent, planning,
sacrifice, hard work, and chemistry.

230

To achieve good chemistry, seek a balance
of personality types—some aggressive go-
getters, some motivators and cheerleaders,
some leaders, some followers. Most of all,
recruit people who treat others with respect.

231

A great leader doesn't wait for people to
come to him; the leader must go out to
them. Employees don't enjoy going to the
boss's office, but they feel appreciated when
the boss comes out on the shop floor.

232

Make sure your message is
simple and memorable.

233

Insecure people use big words and technical jargon to make themselves seem smarter or more important. Communicate in simple terms, not to impress but to be understood.

234

Great communicators are great simplifiers.

235

The best plan is a simple plan.

236

Prepare for the unexpected catastrophe.
Foresee the "unforeseeable."

237

Consistency may not be flashy, but
consistency produces success.

238

Customers don't like surprises. A single
disappointing experience could send your
customer to your competitor—forever.

239

Maintain a high standard of quality.
Consistency is the key to success.

240

Don't just satisfy your
customers—*wow* them.

241

If you deliver more than is expected,
your customers will become your
most effective salespeople.

242

Make people feel special. Call them by
name. Ask their opinion. Treat customers
as honored guests. Show them you
care about them and their needs.

243

After every game, Bill Veeck would stand
at the gate and personally thank people
for coming to the games. I followed
his example from my earliest days as a
minor-league baseball general manager.
I still practice that policy today.

244

There are no unimportant people,
no small roles. Prepare your subs
as well as your starters.

245

Prepare well for the disasters you
expect. Prepare even *more* thoroughly
for the disasters you don't expect.

246

As a leader, prepare your people well—
then step back and watch them succeed.

247

In 1980, when I was general manager of the Philadelphia 76ers, we drafted Andrew Toney. He decided to hold out for more money, claiming he was thinking of grad school instead of the NBA.

Toney was good at basketball, but how good was he at poker? I decided to phone him and find out. I did most of the talking. Andrew did most of the stammering.

"Andrew," I said, "I was hoping to welcome you to the team, but I see you're serious about grad school. So I wish you luck and hope you have a great life."

Moments after I hung up, Andrew's attorney called. "I don't know what you told him," he said, "but it worked. Andrew and I will be in your office in the morning."

248

Great ideas often come from
unexpected sources, including
mailroom clerks and secretaries.

249

I'm a great talker, but I've had to *learn*
to sharpen my listening skills.

250

I didn't become a delegator by
choice. I was forced to trust other
people to get the job done.

251

I had to give up my obsessive control over the details. Why? Because with each new promotion, I acquired more responsibilities and a bigger job description.

252

You cannot know all the operational details that your people on the front lines know.

253

Keep decision-making processes as
simple as possible, and give trusted
subordinates the power to manage
details and solve front-line problems.

254

If you recruit and train your people well,
then trust them to do their jobs, you'll
have many victories to celebrate.

255

The biggest barrier to delegating is fear.
People think, *If I let other people do these
things, I'll become expendable.* Nonsense.
Delegating enables you to get more done—
and that makes you look like a genius!

256

To be a success, hire the best and
brightest—and trust them to do their
job. When they perform brilliantly,
they will make *you* shine.

257

A boss who is a control freak cannot delegate and cannot let go of the petty details. He drives his best people crazy—or worse, drives them to his competitors.

258

In sports, you quickly learn there are factors you can control and factors over which you have *no* control.

259

Welcome dissent. Open communication
requires that people feel free to
express themselves, reasonably and
respectfully, without fear of reprisal.

260

Be tolerant of unconventional ideas.
Don't insist on one way of doing things.

261

I'm excited about every speech I'm about to give, every book I'm about to write, every marathon I'm about to run. The *rest* of my life is the *best* of my life.

262

Focus on results, not rules.

13

People

263

There are no unimportant
people in the world.

264

One of the greatest assets for getting along
with people is a cheerful disposition.

265

We owe each other the simple gift of
kind words and common courtesy.

266

Treating others with respect and kindness
is a simple yet powerful way of using
our words as an influence for good.

267

Class is dignity, good taste, good
manners, and a touch of elegance.

268

To have class is to have confidence in every social situation. It's the ability to relate to everyone, from kings and queens to scrubwomen and ditch-diggers.

269

Always protect the reputation of your friends. Never break a confidence. Never gossip. When others criticize friends in your presence, speak up and defend them.

270

What problems can you solve for others? With others as your consistent focus, you will find yourself becoming more consistently successful.

271

Serve others for the joy of serving, expecting nothing in return. If we "serve" out of a selfish motive, we aren't helping others—we're just helping ourselves.

272

Don't save eulogies for funerals.
Whatever needs to be said, *say it now*.
Tomorrow might be too late.

273

Friends bring out the best in each other.

274

Conflict is a part of life. You can't get
away from it—especially if you are in
leadership. Well-managed conflict can often
be a catalyst for growth and creativity.

275

Dynamic tension is healthy. Different
points of view help us learn, change,
and grow. Our goal is not to eliminate
conflict, but to manage it.

276

We can't always control what we feel, but
we can learn to control our behavior.

277

Don't direct your anger at the other person, but at the problem. State your feelings in a way that respects the other person's feelings and human dignity.

278

A common flashpoint in disagreements is the generalized accusation: "You're *always* so stubborn," or, "You *never* do anything right." What is a person supposed to do with a comment like that?

279

During disagreements, be pinpoint-specific: "I needed that report by three o'clock yesterday. I lost the deal because I didn't have the figures from your department." When you focus on specific behavior instead of a broadside assault on someone's character, the other person is more likely to change that behavior.

280

Keep your words soft and sweet.
You may have to eat them.

281

No argument should ever be bigger than
our commitment to one another.

282

To edify means to *build someone up*. The
term comes from the same root as *edifice*,
a building. To impact people with our
influence, we must build them up.

283

A handwritten note can be treasured,
read again and again, and can
even be suitable for framing.

284

Always praise in public and
criticize in private.

285

Gossip destroys families, churches,
teams, and organizations. It erodes
morale and disrupts relationships.

286

If we set an example of only spreading
"good gossip," of only speaking well of
others, we'll have a healthy influence.
If we spread malicious gossip, we are
poisoning our own well and destroying
our influence with others.

287

Words spoken in a whisper often
return like thunder. Make sure the
words you speak are words you'll be
pleased to hear again someday.

288

People who smile on the outside are more optimistic and enthused on the inside.

289

Make a habit of saying, "I love you." Life is too short to take loved ones for granted.

14

Problem-Solving

290

Life would be boring without
problems to solve.

291

Never run from problems. Face them
squarely. As Robert Frost observed,
"The best way *out* is always *through*."

292

Break problems down into bite-sized
chunks. Don't try to digest them all at once.

293

Battling adversity makes us feel alive and
engaged with the adventure of living.

294

Whatever you face, the real battle is not
"out there" somewhere. It's within you.

295

You begin solving your problems the
moment you accept responsibility for them.

296

Resourcefulness is the ability to apply
imaginative solutions to difficult problems.

297

A good sense of humor keeps
our minds lubricated so we don't
freeze up under pressure.

298

Your problems are outside of you.
What counts is what's inside—your
spirit, your soul, your attitude.

299

Life is a never-ending exercise
in problem-solving.

300

When you reduce a problem to its
essence, the solution becomes clear.

301

Insight can't be taught—but it can be learned by experience. It's the ability to develop keen, accurate hunches based on fragmentary information that the mind processes at an unconscious level.

302

Once, when I lived in Chicago, I had lunch with my pastor, Dr. Warren Wiersbe. After pouring out my problems, I expected sympathy from him. Instead, he seemed absolutely cheerful! "Now, Pat," he said, "don't waste your sufferings. Life is full of problems, so you might as well put them to good use."

303

Insight is the capacity to see beyond surface
appearances to the true nature of a problem.

304

Imagination is the ability to see
beyond what is to what could be.

305

A creative mind is uninhibited and free.

306

Problems are inevitable, but
they are also temporary.

307

The satisfaction of meeting life's
challenges lasts a lifetime.

15

Reading and
Lifelong Learning

308

Surround yourself with the greatness
of the ages. Study great lives.

309

Read good books. The power of
books is absolutely amazing.

310

In a book, an author records a rich slice
of his own experience—his thoughts,
his feelings, his soul—and records
it in lasting symbols on paper.

311

When you open a book, you see into the
heart of another human being—and you
are forever changed by the encounter.

312

A library is a collection of wise friends,
mentors, counselors, and encouragers.
Books instruct and entertain. Books
affect the course of our lives.

313

In books, we find the lives of great leaders,
successful entrepreneurs, brilliant thinkers,
and people of action. Through the magic
of books, we experience thousands of
lives, time-travel through history, and
explore an infinite array of ideas.

314

I read roughly 300 books a year. I
never go anywhere without a book.

315

I've noticed that when I go to a doctor's
office or an airport lounge, the majority
of people sit staring at the floor or texting
on their phones, but hardly anyone
reads. Why would people prefer to sit
and space out instead of engaging heart,
mind, and soul with a fascinating book?

316

Read a book a week. That's 52 books
a year or 520 books over a decade.
Imagine how big your brain will
be after ingesting 520 books!

317

Books increase your vocabulary,
expand your knowledge, increase your
critical thinking skills, and make you
a wiser, more interesting person.

318

When you *purchase* a book, you make a financial investment. When you *read* it, you invest your time and your life. Invest wisely.

319

According to the American Booksellers Association, 80 percent of Americans have not read or purchased even one book during the past twelve months. The average American is not a reader. No wonder he's so average!

320

I enjoy browsing among books and thumbing through them. Scanning the pages, I can get a quick sense of whether the book "speaks" to me or not.

321

Never "kill time." *Fill* your time with a good book. Keep a book with you wherever you go.

322

Whenever you are introduced to someone new, here's a great conversation starter: "What books are you reading?" or "Who is your favorite author?" You can find out more about a person from the books they read than any other way.

323

I read voraciously, compulsively, hungrily. My life has been shaped by books.

324

Ever troubled with insomnia?
Keep a book by your bed.

325

Do you ever have to spend time
"on hold" with your ear stuck to the
phone? Read while you wait.

326

Pick up a book and you can engage in
a dialogue with a great mind that lived
a hundred or a thousand years ago.

327

Don't just read books—interact with them. Argue with them. Wrestle with them. Highlight passages that spark your thinking or challenge your beliefs.

328

Fine books are worth keeping and re-reading.

329

Successful people have voracious minds. They listen, learn, and apply their knowledge to ever-changing situations.

330

The more I learn, the more I discover
how much I don't know.

331

The best way to learn is to ask questions.

332

Asking questions is a sign of
curiosity, humility, and maturity—
hallmarks of a successful person.

333

Shove your eye up against the keyhole of life. Explore the mysteries of the universe.

334

When you learn a new skill, you tilt the playing field a little more in your favor.

335

Not all ideas are equal. Use what
works, discard what doesn't.

336

Successful people listen to others,
but know their own minds.

16

Simplicity and
the Little Things

337

Little things add up. Cumulatively, they become the extra edge that spells the difference between "good" and "great."

338

If you want to build a reputation for quality, start with the little things.

339

The best answer to any critic is success.
And simplicity is the key to success.

340

Complexity produces confusion.
Simplicity produces clarity.

341

Eliminate as many complex variables as you
can. Leave complexity to your opponent.

342

To be victorious, keep it simple.

343

Simplicity is one of the keys to success in basketball and in life.

344

Coach Vince Lombardi had a genius for simplicity. He began every training camp with a team meeting. He'd hold up a football and say, "Gentlemen, this is a football."

345

Leaders must be simplifiers, especially
when they communicate.

346

The fundamentals are simple
to understand—that's why
they're called fundamentals. But
applying the fundamentals takes
commitment and self-discipline.

347

Keep it simple. Drill and rehearse basic
skills until they become instinctive.

348

Prepare for success. The key to preparation
is paying attention to the little things.

349

Show how brilliant you *really* are
through your mastery of simplicity.

350

"Simple" doesn't mean "easy." Most
of the problems we face have simple
solutions, but we are reluctant to make
the sacrifices needed to solve them.

351

If we perfect one "little thing," it probably won't make much difference. But if we perfect many "little things," the cumulative effect becomes great over time.

352

Huge goals are intimidating. But if we tell ourselves, "Let's break this goal down into little tasks," it becomes manageable—and fear evaporates.

353

Little things accumulate over time
to make a big difference.

354

Walt Disney dreamed on the grandest
scale imaginable, yet he always paid
attention to the tiniest details.

355

Excellence is a matter of attention to detail.

356

Tiny details can spell the difference
between success and failure.

357

If we are faithful in the little things, we
will never be beaten by the big things.

17

Time

358

People say, "Someday, when I have more time—" But most of us will never have more time than we have right now. Whatever you want to accomplish, do it now.

359

The best way to control your day is to seize the day and seize it early. Early risers get a jump on the world.

360

Our lives are filled to the bursting point
with things that don't matter—and then we
wonder why we have no time for the things
that *do* matter, such as family time and
fellowship with God. To have a satisfying
life, clear out the clutter and simplify.

361

Successful people value their
time, and they appreciate it when
you value their time as well.

362

Prayer adds time to busy schedules.
Prayer helps us order our priorities.

363

It's okay to say no when people
intrude on your time. You don't
owe anyone an explanation.

364

What will you do with the finite amount
of time that remains for you?

365

Life is precious. Time is irreplaceable.
You don't have a moment to lose.

Sources
of Quotations

A Lifetime of Success

16, 17, 18, 36, 38, 40, 41, 42, 43, 44, 47, 51, 52, 53,
54, 65, 66, 67, 68, 69, 70, 72, 74, 85, 90, 94, 97, 101,
106, 114, 115, 116, 117, 118, 145, 151, 152, 154, 155,
156, 157, 160, 161, 162, 163, 164, 165, 182, 188, 202,
203, 204, 205, 223, 224, 225, 227, 228, 230, 231, 248,
249, 250, 251, 255, 256, 257, 258, 259, 263, 264, 267,
268, 274, 275, 276, 277, 278, 279, 280, 281, 290, 291,
293, 294, 295, 296, 297, 298, 299, 301, 302, 303, 304,
305, 306, 307, 308, 326, 329, 330, 331, 332, 333, 335,
336, 360, 362.

Ahead of the Game

7, 8, 9, 10, 37, 39, 46, 48, 49, 50, 59, 60, 63, 71, 84, 89, 93, 104, 105, 107, 108, 112, 113, 119, 120, 121, 122, 123, 135, 136, 138, 139, 140, 148, 149, 150, 158, 159, 175, 176, 179, 180, 206, 207, 208, 210, 211, 222, 229, 247, 261, 309, 310, 311, 323.

Coach Wooden

15, 21, 22, 23, 64, 78, 79, 80, 81, 82, 111, 137, 220, 269, 271, 272, 273, 312, 313, 314, 315, 316, 317, 318, 319, 320, 321, 322, 324, 325, 327, 328, 358, 363, 365.

Coach Wooden's Greatest Secret

11, 12, 13, 14, 20, 24, 25, 26, 27, 28, 29, 30, 31, 32, 33, 34, 35, 45, 55, 56, 57, 58, 61, 62, 83, 110, 124, 125, 126, 127, 128, 129, 130, 131, 132, 133, 134, 141, 142, 143, 144, 146, 147, 153, 166, 167, 168, 169, 170, 171, 172, 173, 174, 177, 178, 197, 198, 216, 221, 226, 232, 233, 234, 235, 236, 237, 238, 239, 240, 241, 242, 243,

244, 245, 246, 252, 253, 254, 260, 262, 270, 288, 289, 292, 300, 334, 337, 338, 339, 340, 341, 342, 343, 344, 345, 346, 347, 348, 349, 350, 351, 352, 353, 354, 355, 356, 357, 359, 361.

The Difference You Make

1, 2, 3, 4, 5, 6, 19, 73, 75, 76, 77, 86, 87, 88, 91, 92, 95, 96, 98, 99, 100, 102, 103, 109, 181, 183, 184, 185, 186, 187, 189, 190, 191, 192, 193, 194, 195, 196, 199, 200, 201, 209, 212, 213, 214, 215, 217, 218, 219, 265, 266, 282, 283, 284, 285, 286, 287, 364.

Pat Williams is senior vice president of the NBA's Orlando Magic. He has almost fifty years of professional sports experience, has written over seventy books, and is one of America's most sought-after motivational speakers.

Jim Denney is a writer with more than eighty books to his credit. His collaborative titles include *Reggie White in the Trenches, Undefeated,* and numerous books with Pat Williams.

CONNECT WITH PAT

We would love to hear from you. Please send your comments about this book to Pat Williams:

pwilliams@orlandomagic.com

Pat Williams
c/o Orlando Magic
8701 Maitland Summit Boulevard
Orlando, FL 32810

If you would like to set up a speaking engagement for Pat, please contact his assistant, Andrew Herdliska:
(407) 916-2401
aherdliska@orlandomagic.com

PATWILLIAMS.COM

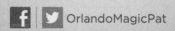 OrlandoMagicPat

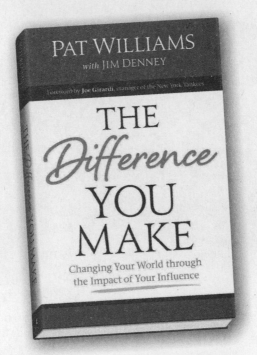

GOOD MAN,
GREAT COACH

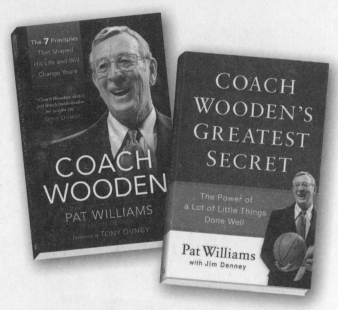

Pat Williams shares wisdom and experience from the
legendary Coach Wooden that could **change your life**.